EVERYTHING ABOUT SEWING
PANTS &
JUMPSUITS
FROM VOGUE PATTERNS

Editor
Patricia Perry
Technical Coordinator
Elizabeth Musheno
Art Directors
Jean-Jacques Du Bane
Elizabeth Shurter
Copy Editor
Norma Risman
Artists
Karen Coughlin
Gisela Sachs

CONTENTS

Pants People...All Of Us!

The tall and the short and the stout! We're all into pants these days! Evenings, too! The '70s see them as a mainstay of feminine wardrobes . . . totally fashion-right everywhere, any time, for any occasion. And happily, there's hardly a woman among us who can't wear pants, in one style or another . . . and look just great in them!

The secret of successful pant-dressing? Same as with all your other clothes! Namely: choosing those that flatter your figure assets and conceal your figure faults.

"Know thyself" is the all-important motto! Let it be your guide. Make your own very personal figure analysis before a full length mirror. And don't neglect the rear view! Wearing only your undergarments, locate your figure discrepancies. Do you have a small waist and broad hips? Do you sort of billow out in front . . . or carry a caboose? Take a truthful inventory. And don't worry about the findings. The more imperfections, the more "normal" you are! And with all the myriad pant styles available, you're going to find those that specifically flatter YOUR figure, fool the public, and make you look sensational!

The many shapes and sizes among us fall, generally, into four major figure categories. Let's consider each of these, along with pointers for successful pant wearing:

The Tall, Ramrod-Thin Figure wears pants especially well. Any pants! Enjoy 'em all! Accent your naturally long, lean look with body jumpsuits or ensembles in soft, clingy fabrics. To fill out a thin figure, choose full-bodied, richly textured or boldly patterned fabrics. Layering on separates will also add substance to a too-thin frame. For example:

pull a sweater down hip-low over your pants, and top it all off with a long vest of luscious, thick fabric.

Want to cut your height? Consider crosswise stripes . . . pants and tops in contrast . . . a wide, important belt. In fitting the too-thin figure, remember that pants should not be so tight that they reveal too-willowy legs . . . nor so loose that baggy wrinkles tattle on your lack of curves. Concentrate on perfecting the fit of your pants so that they show off an enviably sleek silhouette: YOURS!

The Short, Thin Will-o-the-Wisp type can look taller in outfits that are all one bright 'n lively color . . . and look curvier in lightly textured fabrics, medium plaids, checks or prints. Avoid clingy fabrics which reveal your lack of natural curves.

The all-in-one jumpsuit is a great idea for you . . . perhaps one with pockety detail to add dimension to your slender figure. High, collared necklines are top flattery . . . while slightly flared pantlegs are good shapemakers. With shorter-length pants, extend the color line downward from the hemline via matching hose and shoes, or matching boots.

Remember that proportion is the key to your most successful pant looks. Don't have the top portion of your outfit too long or too short . . . do find the balance between the two that is pleasing to your eye. And keep accessories in scale: don't let an over-sized shoulder bag obliterate your bodice, or a chunky chain belt weigh you down.

The Tall, Amply Endowed Woman with avoirdupois at bust, waist, hip or thigh is included in the pants picture. If you are in this category, avoid like the plague any pant look that might add extra bumps or bulges. Concentrate on pattern styles and fabrics that create a slimming effect. Look for pants patterns with smooth, back-seam zipper clos-

ings . . . or elasticized waistbands . . . and pantlegs that fall straight or flare easily from hip to heel. Disguise extra pounds with skims of lightweight, firm-bodied fabrics . . . all in one rich, but subdued color. Fit lightly over heavy areas, as thighs or waist, to avoid a "packed-in" look. Fluff or ruffles, too-tiny prints, snug-fitting belts . . . all no-nos for you!

And practice the principles of proportion in balancing your figure. For instance: if you're bottom-heavy, plan a pants outfit with bodice detail that draws the eye up and away from prominent hips. Keep accessories in proportion, too: no bitsy little bags or fragile-looking shoes to upset the balance of a great total look!

The Short, Curvaceous Woman may have had the idea that she is "not the pants type." Not true! Well-fitting pants, in the right style and fabric, can add inches to your height . . . and streamline curves, too! Choose styles with simple, vertical lines . . . straight legs . . . easy, unrevealing fit. Pantlegs made without side seams will eliminate fabric bulk over the outer thigh, and provide a slick, front-creased trouser shape.

Select lightweight, smooth surfaced fabrics. Staying all-one-color from top to toe is a slimming trick. So is the use of narrow lengthwise stripes. Your ideal pant look might well be a two-piece garment with a top that drops easily from shoulder to hip and ends slightly below the crotch—thus concealing a multitude of figure sins.

Choose jumpsuits that are only semi-fitting. Avoid up-tight necklines . . . and all but the narrowest of belts. A flat, shoulder-slung bag will accent the long, lean look.

WHATEVER your figure type, take the time to study yourself, to plan your personal pants strategy. It will be time well spent!

The Many Moods of Pants

The pants approach to fashion offers Today's woman new freedom of choice in dressing for every occasion. And an endlessly exciting choice it is! From it, select the silhouettes and fabric interpretations that flatter YOU . . . that best express your individualism . . . and accord with your personal life style.

You can go to town in debonair pantsuits . . . tailored in luxe wools, twills or linen weaves. Or travel the world over in pant turnouts of wonderfully wiltless double knits.

Make it on the job in the "pants-plus" of separates that can mix it up for a 5-day week of fashion. (With pants plus sweaters, shirts, vests, cardigan tops . . . and more!)

Or take to the country life! Rush back to nature in pants of rustic tweed . . . a jersey jump . . . "working" denim jeans. Run off to the sun in Jamaicas or boy-shorts that keep their cool in crisp cottons and carefree blends. Sail away in see-worthy deck pants, knee-high in canvas, duck or poplin.

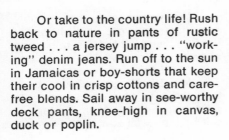

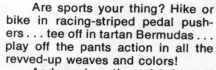

Are sports your thing? Hike or bike in racing-striped pedal pushers . . . tee off in tartan Bermudas . . . play off the pants action in all the revved-up weaves and colors!

And see how those fabrics call the tune! How your favorite pant-look legs it in a campus plaid . . . goes city-chic in gabardine . . . goes gala in brocade!

Let the many pant moods add new dimension to your fashion life! Your fashion image, too! Go gaucho in a dashing leather look or a jungle print. Get your knicker kicks in anything from tweed to velveteen.

For the festive nights, be sensuous in a jumpsuit slink of nylon knit or velvet. Be dramatic in a Pucci pant-sweep of spectacular print. Be feminine in a drift of flowering silk culottes. Be bold and baring in the shortest satin shortpants! Make little evenings at home big events in leisure-loving pants—and softly sensational fabrics!

Got the picture? Be YOURSELF . . . in the fresh fashion excitement of pant dressing!

The Long and The Short of It

The dictionary defines trousers as "any garment which covers each leg separately." The fashion definition of Today's many trouser looks is considerably more exciting! It begins by encompassing two distinct categories: **pants,** which begin at the waist . . . and **jumpsuits,** which begin at the shoulders. Both categories embrace exciting variations of silhouette.

Length, perhaps more than anything else, distinguishes the many styles and types of pants on the fashion scene. So we'll divide our definition into groups governed by length —and give you the long and short of the going styles found in pants as well as jumpsuits.

Classic . . . Full Length

These are the pants that hover around the instep . . . and leg it in countless fashion ways!

The fit is usually snug around the hips, sometimes softened with front waistline pleats. Waistlines may be natural, raised or dropped. But ah, the legs!

Pantlegs may be tubular **stovepipes . . . straight** and trouser-creased . . . **flared** from the hip or **bell-bottom** flared from the knee . . . or **downhill-tapered,** as in ski pants.

Elephant pants are wide-cut, full and flowing. **Jeans** are spare and skinny, with a pocketed, top-stitched "working" look. **Gangster pants** go straight, but wide and floppy; they're usually cuffed, and often have front waistline pleats which extend into the extra fullness straight down the leg. **Cuffed** pant-legs turn up in almost any Classic variation. Then there are **hipsters** that ride low, sometimes minus a waistband; they are usually, but not necessarily, Classic in length.

STOVE PIPES

STRAIGHT

JUMPSUIT/BELL-BOTTOM

TAPERED SKI PANTS

8

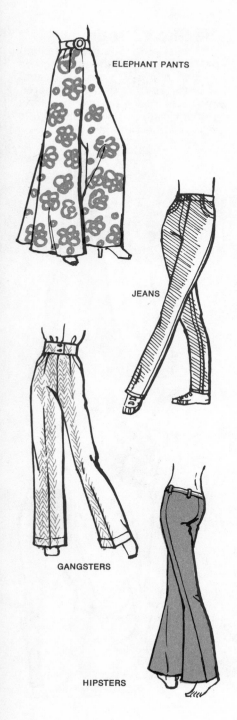

ELEPHANT PANTS

JEANS

GANGSTERS

HIPSTERS

Stylized Mid-Lengths

This category includes a variety of pant looks in shorter-than-long lengths. All are extremely wearable . . . versatile, too—qualities that add up to standout fashion appeal and popularity.

Important among this gathering are **culottes,** or **pantskirts**—all with the look of skirts, but providing the greater freedom of pants. Stylewise, these may be tailored, pleated or flared . . . and range in length from breezy, above-the-knee to mid-calf fashion levels.

Gaucho pants—named for the South American cowboys who originally wore this trouser style—are basically a culotte-type garment, but are not designed to look like a skirt. Often banded at the waist, they flare dashingly from snug-fitting hips to wide hemlines somewhere below the knee.

CULOTTE/PANTSKIRT

GAUCHOS

9

Capri pants fit close to the calf and skinny down to a few inches short of the ankle. **Pedal pushers** make it to mid-calf . . . shaping up as chopped-off classic pants. **Bootleggers** or **deck pants** are rolled up or cuffed to the knee. **Knickers** start with a classic pant silhouette, but stop just below the knee. The lower edge is then gathered to a band, or casing-finished, to pull in the fullness that blouses over the knees.

The Short Crops

These varied short styles climb up from the knee. **Bermuda** length is about 2″ above . . . closely related **Jamaicas** go to mid-thigh. Tailored **boy-shorts** and girly, whirly **skorts** rise thigh-high . . . while **shortpants** are as short as the law allows!

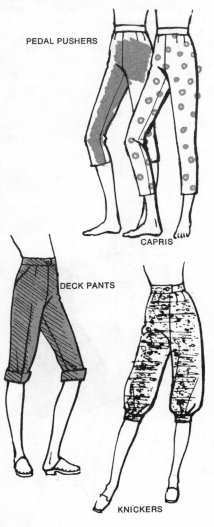

PEDAL PUSHERS

CAPRIS

DECK PANTS

KNICKERS

BERMUDAS

JAMAICAS

SKORT

BOY-SHORTS

SHORTPANTS

Master Planning

Before your pants can start to take shape, there's a bit of groundwork to be done. Get to know your figure. Study the pros and cons of pattern selection . . . and the fabrics that will make the most of it. In short: make your master plan for great pants-to-be!

The Fashion Measure of Pants

The key to handsome pants and jumpsuits is perfect fit. To achieve it, you must first obtain accurate measurements of your figure.

Begin by putting on the undergarments you intend to wear with your pants. Be sure to select those which are not too tight, as you want a smooth contour unmarred by bumps or bulges. Also, put on the type of shoes you will wear with your pants. Take your measurements in front of a mirror—or call in a close friend to help you measure hard-to-reach territory. Be accurate . . . be honest . . . and record all evidence on a chart, as you take these measurements:

Waist: Tie a string around the body so it settles comfortably at the waist. Measure your waist at the string (1). (Note: leave string in place to facilitate further measurements taken from waist.)

High Hip: Measure across top of hip bones 2″ to 4″ below waist (2).

Full Hip: Measure the fullest part of your hips. Vogue places this hipline approximately 7″-9″ from the waist, depending on size range (3).

Circumference of Leg: Measure fullest part of thigh (4), knee (5), calf (6), and instep (7).

Length: Measure at side from waist to center of knee (8), waist to calf (9), and waist to floor or desired long length (10).

Crotch Length: Sit on a hard chair and measure from the side waist to the chair seat (11).

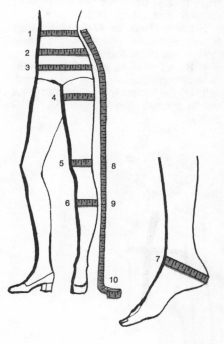

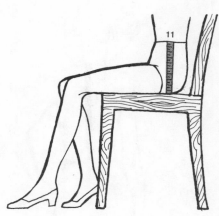

If you plan to make a jumpsuit, you will also want a record of your upper body dimensions—to combine with your pants data. The most important of these are:

Bust: Measure over fullest part of bust and straight across back (12).

Front Neck to Waist: Measure from hollow between neck bones to center front waistline (13).

Back Neck to Waist: Measure from prominent back neck bone down center back to waist (14).

If you wish to include more detailed "top" statistics on your chart, follow the complete measurement guide given in the VOGUE SEWING BOOK.

Keep your completed chart close at hand throughout your pants-making. It will be your constant reference in making adjustments and achieving perfect fit. And as time goes by, keep it up to date—recording any measurement differentials which may occur with weight changes.

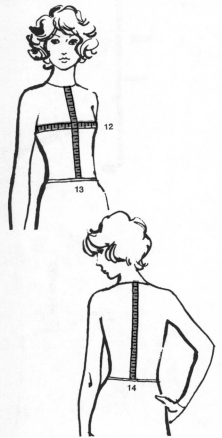

My Measurements		
Date		
Weight		
Inches		
1 Waist		
2 High hip		
3 Full hip		
4 Thigh		
5 Knee		
6 Calf		
7 Instep		
8 Length waist to knee		
9 Length waist to calf		
10 Length waist to floor		
11 Crotch length		
12 Bust		
13 Front neck to waist		
14 Back neck to waist		

Pick Your Pattern Size

After you have made a complete analysis of your figure and taken accurate measurements, you're prepared to purchase your pattern in your correct size. Look to the size and measurement chart in the Vogue catalog, or on the pattern envelope back, for guidance.

For pants, we recommend you select the pattern size that accords with your waist measurement. However, if your hip is larger than that paired with the pattern waist size—select your pattern by hip measurement. Why? Because the waistline adjustment will be much easier to do than a hip-fitting correction would be.

On the other hand, most jumpsuit patterns should be purchased according to the bust measurement, because this area is the hardest to alter when dealing with an all-in-one garment.

Another important measurement to check when picking a jumpsuit pattern is your back neck-to-waist

length . . . which will aid in determining whether your figure type is a Misses, Junior, Womens, Half Size or Miss Petite.

Probably not all of your measurements will coincide with those on the pattern envelope . . . but they will serve as a starting point for both pattern selection and alteration. If you fall between two pattern sizes, study your body structure to determine the correct one for you. Small-boned gals should choose the smaller of two sizes . . . large-boned ladies will need the larger size.

Remember that the measurements listed on the pattern envelope are BODY SIZES, and that additional ease has been built in to allow for free movement, comfort, and any softness dictated by the design.

An exception to this occurs in Vogue patterns that are specified for "stretchable knits" only. In these instances, the pattern has been designed and sized with the premise that the stretchable knit will, in itself, provide the necessary ease. Also, such patterns usually do not allow for linings or underlinings . . . and the finished garment is intended to fit close to the body.

The important point, in every case, is to CHOOSE YOUR PATTERN SIZE BY THE LISTED BODY MEASUREMENTS.

If you are about to make your first pair of pants, we suggest you select a simply styled pattern. However, don't be hesitant about your pants project for fear it may be difficult. Actually, pants and jumpsuits are probably the easiest of all garments to construct . . . especially after you have learned about your figure from a muslin fitting shell (see pages 20-24). And with a bit of experience you may find it takes considerably less time to MAKE pants than to find good-fitting ones in ready-to-wear.

Choose Your Fashion Fabric

There is not a single type of fabric sold today that is not suitable for either pants or jumpsuits if handled correctly! The main consideration is how well your pattern style and fabric work together. And how they combine to produce figure flattery and a fashion-right look for You!

For example, a thin, soft fabric will cling closer to the leg than a fabric with more body. It would be best in a pants style with a slightly wider leg. Just the opposite is true for a very firm fabric, which would be cumbersome in a full-cut pantleg—but ideal for slim or straightleg trousers.

In selecting your fabric, examine it carefully . . . drape it over your leg . . . see how it behaves with underlining fabric. Is it woven or knitted? This structure difference will greatly affect the fall of the finished garment. Most knits, unless bonded, will be more figure revealing than woven fabrics . . . a fact to keep in mind when choosing your pattern style AND your fabric.

Also, consider the surface of your fabric. Often, textures or motifs can establish a fashion mood in translating your pattern design. A perfect example is denim—almost synonymous with sportswear. Or, choose a lush velveteen—and you're well on your way to a party pant-look.

But just because most fabrics can be made into pants doesn't mean that each is suitable for all! Certain textures, weights and weaves lend themselves to particular designs—and you must determine which is the most appropriate for the pants you plan to make. Crisp, flat fabrics tailor very well—while soft, supple fabrics are the ones to choose for clinging feminine looks.

Plaids or stripes can make a simple outfit distinctive and eye-catching. If you plan to include one of these motifs in your scheme of things, be sure—first of all—to select a pattern that's suitable. Check the fabric information and recommendations on the back of the pattern envelope or on the catalog page. If your pattern is not recommended for plaids, or stripes, these motifs will never properly match at the seams, or form chevron effects—no matter how hard you work at it.

If your pattern is suitable for plaids or uneven stripes, be sure to purchase extra yardage to allow for matching them in the construction of your outfit. Base your estimate of this extra fabric on your pattern size, the size of the plaid or stripe repeat, and the number of lengths of the major pattern pieces.

Prints—all kinds—can be used for both pants and jumpsuits. However, if you choose a large or definitely spaced print, it's also wise to allow extra yardage for the proper placement of these motifs in your pattern layout.

And lastly, allow a bit of extra yardage if you expect to lengthen your pattern to accord with your height.

When it comes to buying your fabric, don't skimp on these additional few inches which may be needed. Better to be safe than sorry! You can always use any left-over fabric for patchwork, or something . . . but there is NOTHING so frustrating as finding yourself long on pattern and short on fabric while cutting out your prospective garment!

...And Your Inner Fabrics

Pants and jumpsuits are not the usual garments we associate with inner fabrics. However, the use of these materials depends upon the character of your fashion fabric and your pants design.

Underlining is the inner fabric with which you are probably most familiar. Essentially, it lends subtle shaping and support. It reduces wrinkling. And it can add to the life of your garment by protecting the fashion fabric from inner abrasion.

Underlining is desirable for many woven fabrics—but is not needed for knits, which have a degree of stretchability that you do not wish to inhibit. What you must evaluate is whether or not the features of underlining are important to the final success of your pants or jumpsuit.

It's particularly important to take into consideration the marking and stitching which your outer fabric requires. When an underlining is used, all the regular construction markings and symbols will be noted on it—and you avoid the risk of marking an expensive or delicate fashion fabric. Probably the strongest argument for using underlining in pants is its ability to act as a "hanger" for the garment. In this capacity, all facings, interfacings and hems can be sewn in place without the stitches showing on the outside.

Select your underlining according to its purpose. Test it with your outer fabric, draping the two over your hand to see if they complement each other. Try different weights for different effects: very soft, if mainly intended to support stitches . . . firm, if it is to give shape and body to a fashion fabric.

Interfacing is used to give support and stability to stress areas . . . to prevent stretching . . . to add body or crispness without bulk. It is most often found in the waistband area of pants, at the neckline or down the front of jumpsuits. It may also be used at the hemline of some pants, to maintain the shape of a fuller lower edge.

When your pattern calls for interfacing, select one that is somewhat lighter in weight than the garment fabric. Choose it according to the function it will perform. A firmly woven type is recommended for stabilizing buttonholes, while a flexible, all-bias non-woven will be perfect for the rolled turtle neck of a knit jumpsuit or the hem of a crisp fabric pantleg. Iron-on interfacings are also available, but they should be thoroughly pre-tested with your fabric.

Lining gives pants and jumpsuits a smooth, luxurious custom finish. Like underlining, it prolongs the life of the garment, prevents stretching, reduces wrinkling and helps preserve the shape. Unlike underlining, it should never in any way influence the fit or characteristics of the outer fabric.

Lining is not essential in most closed garments, especially pants, but it can be a "plus" if the fabric is scratchy, clingy, revealing—or apt to go baggy at seat or knees. In the latter case, you may wish to use a partial lining in the front portion of the legs instead of a full lining.

For detailed instructions on inserting these inner fabrics, see pages 30-31 and 41-42.

Pattern Fitting...Personalized

Perfect fit is what makes all the difference between merely "good" pants . . . and GREAT pants! And achieving a flawless fit depends on more than just buying the correct pattern size. The standard body measurements—on which all patterns are based—are simply average body measurements of women within a particular size range. Individuals of each size may vary in any number of ways from these standardizations.

And SHAPES vary! For instance: your hips may be a "perfect 36" . . . but are they shaped wide, leaving you pancake-flat fore and aft . . . or are they narrow, gaining their girth by way of a rounded tummy and derrière? No one pair of pants could fit both of these figures.

So, obviously, the measurements given in your pattern can serve only as the starting point from which you must make adjustments to fit your own very personal dimensions.

If you plan to include varied pant looks in your fashion life, you can ensure a perfect fit in each and every one of them if you first make a muslin fitting shell of pants—complete with all your personalized adjustments.

To make this, select a simply styled fitted pants pattern with straight legs—one which relates to your own body shape and contours. You will use this as the basis for making your muslin pants. And in the final analysis, you'll discover exactly what your own fitting problems are, and exactly how to solve them—before you ever touch shears to your fashion fabric!

Once done, these basic pattern adjustments and muslin alterations can be easily transferred to any pants patterns you choose in the same size. All fitting guesswork will be eliminated . . . and you can work confidently in cutting and sewing all your favorite pant looks. With custom fit every time!

As noted, the whole procedure involves two major steps. First: making preliminary adjustments on a flat basic pattern. Next: working on the actual muslin, shaping it to your own body contours.

Flat Pattern Adjustments

All obvious adjustments of length and circumference should be made on the flat pattern pieces of your basic pants pattern BEFORE YOU CUT YOUR MUSLIN.

Your body measurement chart (see page 12) has all the statistics you need to personalize this pattern . . . and now you are going to interpret some of that information and transfer it onto your pattern pieces. To do this, you'll need a few additional guidelines besides those already printed on your Vogue Pattern. So get a ruler and a triangle, and prepare to draw them in yourself. For starters, extend the grainline markings the full length of all pattern pieces.

Then, as you proceed, observe these important rules of the game:
1) Always measure from seamlines rather than cutting lines.
2) Make all additions and subtractions on both front and back pattern pieces.
3) To shorten: make a tuck one half the width of the excess amount along the adjustment line on the pattern piece. Fasten with tape.
4) To lengthen: cut pattern along the adjustment line, place

tissue paper underneath, and spread to the amount needed. Fasten with tape.

5) To decrease circumference: slim pattern at seam edges, tapering new seamlines and cutting lines to meet original ones.

6) To increase circumference: fasten tissue paper under pattern edge, extending outward. Draw new seamlines and cutting lines as required, tapering to original lines.

Crotch Length: The most important fitting area is the crotch—which is really a series of complex curves. Unless the crotch is in the right place to begin with, no amount of adjustment later can rectify it.

To establish your correct Crotch Length on the pants pattern pieces, place your triangle on the printed grainline in such a manner that it meets the point of the crotch. Draw a line along the top of the triangle, and extend it across the width of the pattern piece. This is your CROTCH LINE.

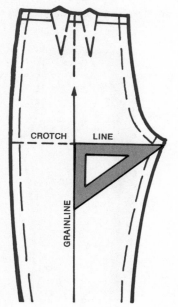

Position Lines: You will need these guidelines for further adjustment and fitting. Add them to your pattern tissue now. Using the chart of your body measurements and their locations (as established on page 11 and 12) as your point of reference—draw these lines on FRONT and BACK pattern pieces.

On the side seam, measure down the established distance from the waistline to your High Hip measurement point (#2); pencil-dot this location. Place a triangle on the printed grainline so that the top crosses your location dot. Draw a line along the top of the triangle and extend it across the width of the pattern. This is your HIGH HIP POSITION LINE.

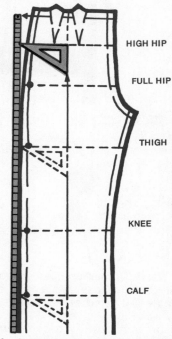

In the same manner, draw position lines for your Full Hip (#3), and your Thigh line (#4)—locating this at the same level at which you measured yourself. Similarly, draw position lines at your Knee length (#8), and Calf length (#9); these will be particularly important guidelines whenever you make shorter length or slim-fitting pants.

Jot your body measurements on the pattern near each position line; this will expedite checking these areas to see if they need adjustment in width.

Crotch Adjustment: Measure the side seam from waist seamline to your established Crotch Line. This length should be the same as your body crotch measurement (#11) plus ½" for sitting ease. If not, lengthen or shorten the pattern pieces, as needed, along the nearby adjustment line. Correct crotch curve.

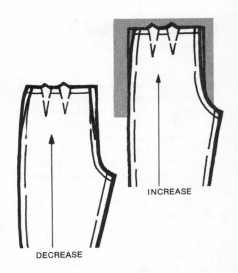

DECREASE

INCREASE

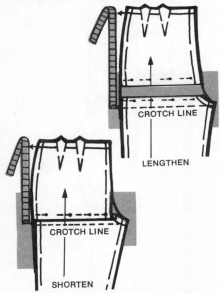

CROTCH LINE

LENGTHEN

CROTCH LINE

SHORTEN

Waist Circumference: Is your waist (body measurement #1) the same as that listed on your pattern? If not—add or slim away ⅛ of the total difference at each center and side seam of the pattern front and back, tapering new lines to the hip level. Be sure to make corresponding adjustments on the waistband or facing pattern pieces.

Hip Circumference: No change should be necessary if your pattern was purchased by hip measurement. However, to adjust pattern to a slightly larger hip measurement, add width at the side seams. Mark ¼ of the amount required opposite the Full Hip position line **and** the pants hemline. Connect these markings, drawing new lines that taper to the waist.

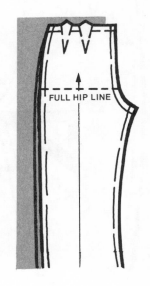

FULL HIP LINE

18

Leg Circumference: Measure the Thigh line, from seam to seam, on the front and back patterns. Add front and back measurements. The total pattern measurement should equal your own thigh (body measurement #4) plus 1″ or 2″ for wearing ease. To increase or decrease the leg width—add or take away ½ of the required amount at the inner leg seam of both the front and the back pattern pieces. (Remember to include the 1″ or 2″ of wearing ease allowance in your adjustment.) Retain the crotch curve by tapering new lines to meet the original ones.

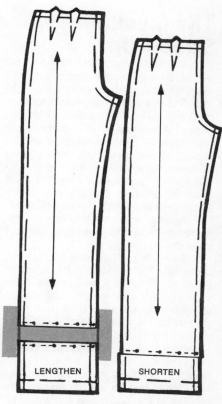

LENGTHEN   SHORTEN

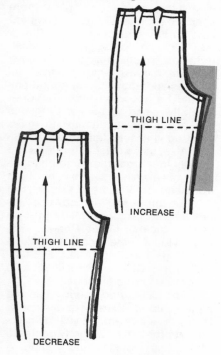

THIGH LINE

INCREASE

THIGH LINE

DECREASE

Pants Length: After any needed crotch adjustment has been made, check the total length of the pants with your body measurement #10—measuring along the side seamline from waist to hemline. Lengthen or shorten, as needed, at the adjustment line above the hemline.

The importance of these personalized adjustments cannot be over-emphasized! As you make them, you will come to understand your figure and your individual fitting problems. As you continue, and make a muslin fitting shell (strongly recommended for those with more complex figure problems) these flat pattern adjustments you have made will put you well on your way toward the successful correction of your more major figure discrepancies. If, however, your figure is fairly normal —you may find that your fitting problems are solved by these minor adjustments. Then, just keep this as your permanent "basic fitting pattern" for pants—and transfer each of the adjustments you have made here to any fashion pants pattern.

The Muslin Shape-Up

To make your pants-fitting shell, select a crisp muslin that won't wilt as you work on it.

Cut out pants according to your adjusted pattern. Transfer all grainlines, seamlines and construction markings to the wrong side of the muslin. (Use a tracing wheel and dressmaker's carbon for the quickest, most permanent method of marking.) Then thread trace the grainlines and the established position lines of your High and Full Hip, Knee and Calf to the right side of your muslin.

Staystitch all curved edges (see page 30). Then machine baste pants together, following the procedure of your pattern's Sewing Guide. Baste a temporary waistband of grosgrain ribbon to the waist seamline to support pants while fitting.

Now try on your muslin pants, and take a critical look in a full length mirror to spot individual fitting problems. Side seams should be perpendicular to the floor. The traced position lines of Hip, Thigh, etc., should be exactly parallel to the floor. If they are pulled or distorted, or if wrinkling occurs, you will need to make some fitting alterations on your muslin. (And remember: for comfort and attractiveness, avoid fitting pants too tightly.)

First check the areas listed below. It may be that the minor alterations recommended will correct any existent problems to your satisfaction:

1) Does the waist pull downward at center front or back when you sit or stand? To correct, set waistband higher at the center seam, tapering to original level at sides.

2) Do pants wrinkle at the High Hipline? To correct, release darts; re-pin to fit body contour, lengthening or shortening darts as needed.

3) Is the thigh area too tight or too baggy? To correct, let out or take in inner leg seam slightly, as needed, from the crotch point downward.

Mark all corrections on your muslin with a contrasting color pencil. You will later want to transfer these alterations to your tissue pattern.

If irregularities of fit persist, it means that you need one of the more specialized alterations to compensate for figure discrepancies. Check the following pages for specific alterations which apply to your body contour requirements. It must be emphasized: these fitting alterations should be accomplished ON YOUR MUSLIN, since additional problems will occur if you attempt to make them on your final fashion fabric.

Also, since these alterations are usually localized, the same changes are not always required on both front and back pattern pieces. But DO remember to make corresponding adjustments on all adjoining seams, facings or waistband. And, as previously noted, carefully MARK ALL DART AND SEAMLINE CORRECTIONS ON YOUR MUSLIN with a contrasting color pencil.

For Large Abdomen: While the pattern hip measurement allows for the girth of this area, it will not compensate for individual body contours that cause wrinkles and pulling. A protruding abdomen can cause pants front to be distorted at the waist and hipline, pulling side seams forward, and wrinkling into "smile lines" at the crotch. However, fabric can be molded smoothly over this area to minimize rather than accent it. To accomplish this: release front waist seam and darts. Drop the pants front until side seams fall straight. Baste fabric strip to top of pants. Re-pin darts to fit contour. Join smooth-fitting top to waistband. To eliminate front crotch wrinkles, add a strip of fabric to the front inner leg seam until pants hang smoothly.

Protruding Hip Bones: These may cause fabric to pull across the front. To correct, release front darts and pin to fit contour—shortening or widening darts, as needed. If this decreases the waistline, add to side seams of front. Re-baste.

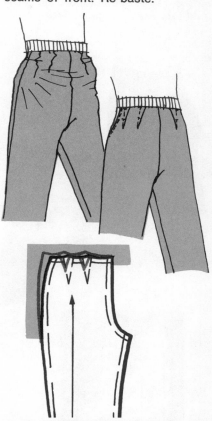

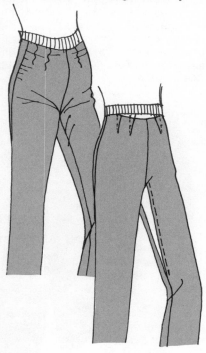

Large Buttocks: Buying your pattern by hip measurement will give you the "coverage" for a large derrière. But wrinkles may form above and below buttocks—and pulling may distort side seams. This simply indicates that you need more length concentrated at the center back to accommodate the generous curve. To achieve this in your muslin, release dart and drop back waistline seam from waistband until side seams fall smoothly. Baste a strip of fabric to pants top. Re-pin darts to fit contour. If the waistline measurement is decreased by this alteration, add to the side seams. Join the re-shaped top to waistband. If pants still draw below the buttocks, add a strip of fabric to back inner leg seam until this area hangs smoothly.

horizontal fold across the high hip-line, or where needed, tapering to side seams . . . and pin a perpendicular fold along the side back of each leg, tapering to nothing at the waist and knee. Re-pin darts to fit body contour; they will become shorter and narrower. Take out excess waistline width at side seam. (Pin the identical perpendicular fold in your tissue pattern later, clipping the side seam allowance so that pattern will lie flat.) Note Back-Fitting Seams, page 23.

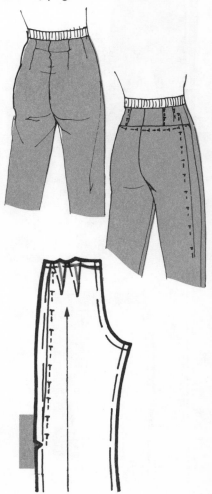

Flat Buttocks: This may leave considerable "empty" space across the back of your muslin pants. You can eliminate most of the wrinkles and bagginess in two strokes: pin a

Sway Back: This common figure or posture fault will cause your pants or jumpsuit to wrinkle below the waistline at back. To correct muslin, pin out wrinkles with a horizontal fold, tapering to side seams. Re-pin darts, which will become shorter as back waistline curve is deepened. (For another remedy, note Back-Fitting Seams below.)

ultra-tight fitting pants!) Simply pin the unwanted back fullness into a seam that extends from waist to hemline, straight down the center back of each leg. This seam should parallel the grainline as closely as possible—though it may vary in depth as it follows the contours of your body. Re-pin darts to conform to your figure. (Mark new seamlines on muslin; unpin, and transfer seam markings to tissue pattern later.)

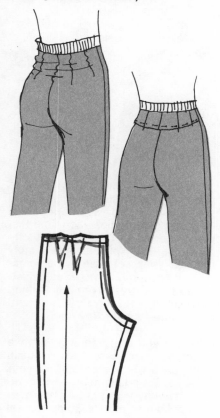

Back-Fitting Seams: One of the world's top designers originated a unique fashion technique for attaining a particularly smooth back fit on pants. You can make his method work for you in eliminating excess back fullness caused by flat buttocks or a swayback. (And this technique is also applicable if you just prefer

After your muslin is perfectly fitted—and all alterations accurately marked—these changes must be transferred to your basic tissue pattern (which will soon become your master pattern). To do this, it's usually necessary to take your muslin fitting shell apart. However, you'll probably find that not all the pattern pieces will need to be changed, as most alterations are done on just the front or the back.

Carefully press the altered muslin piece, and lay it on a flat surface with the completely marked wrong side facing up . . . place your tissue pattern over it . . . and prepare to transfer all the muslin alterations to this master pattern. In doing this, it is most important to remember that the GRAINLINE REMAINS STABLE. So be sure to match the grainline marking of your tissue pattern to the original grainline of your muslin first . . . and pin in place so that un-altered seamlines coincide.

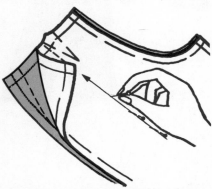

You can now see at a glance, through the tissue, just where your pattern changes will occur . . . where darts, seamlines and cutting lines will be re-drawn. Transfer all these construction changes from your muslin onto your tissue pattern, using a colored pencil for definition —and a ruler and French curve for accuracy.

Your master pants pattern is now perfectly adjusted and fitted to YOU. Make it a permanent sewing tool by mounting the pattern pieces —quickly, easily and ingeniously— on a heavy weight of iron-on, non-woven interfacing fabric (or on heavy paper).

The extra time it has taken to produce your muslin fitting shell and your master pattern will be regained over and over again—each time that you make a pair of pants, a culotte or a jumpsuit. You can now simply transfer your completely personalized and accurately recorded adjustments and alterations to any fashion pattern of your choice . . . and achieve perfect fit every time!

NOTE: If you are planning to make a jumpsuit, you can make a muslin fitting shell which incorporates your usual bodice adjustments—and combine it with your pants shell. Use the bodice of Vogue's Guide to Perfect Fit of Fitted Garments (Pattern #1000) for this purpose. And keep these two important points in mind:

1) Your jumpsuit will require an additional ⅜" of body ease at the back neck-to-waist measurement (for seating stretch).

2) Side seamlines, waist and hip darts must be aligned at the waistline of bodice and pants.

Are You Ready?

After making all necessary adjustments on your selected pattern — according to your muslin fitting shell and master pattern—the Great Moment is approaching! You are getting ready to cut out your pants in your fashion fabric. And it's an important procedure—because as ye cut, so shall ye sew!

Prepare Your Fabric

Steam press carefully to remove "store wrinkles" and fold lines.

Straighten fabric ends by snipping into the selvage, pulling a crosswise thread, and cutting along this line across the entire width.

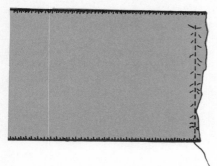

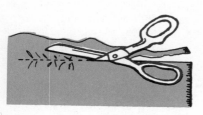

If thread won't pull (as in some tightly woven, nubby or fuzzy fabrics), carefully mark the crosswise thread and cut along marking. In knits, cut along a line of crosswise loops.

Straighten the grain of your fabric; it is vital to the perfect hang of your finished pants. Check this grain accuracy after ends have been evened, by folding fabric lengthwise and pinning the selvages and edges of one end together. If fabric lies flat and smooth on a table, it is on grain. If not, straighten it with steam pressing — stroking firmly from the selvages toward the fold.

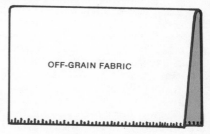

OFF-GRAIN FABRIC

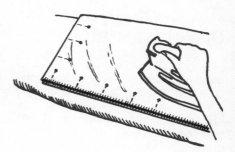

For another way to straighten the grain: remove pins and gently, but firmly, pull fabric on the bias—in the direction opposing the slant of the off-grain lines—until a perfect right angle corner is formed.

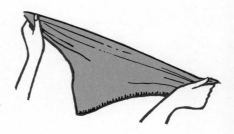

Certain permanent finish fabrics (such as bonded fabrics, some underlinings, and those fabrics which specify this information on hangtags and labels) can never be straightened. It is quite all right to use them as they are—as long as no matching will be required—they usually will not stretch out of shape. To prepare them for cutting, just match and pin the selvages only—and cut the ends so that they form a right angle with the selvage. (Avoid buying a fabric that is printed off grain; it can never be properly matched.)

Shrink your fabric before cutting if hangtag or bolt-end message specifies more than 1% residual shrinkage . . . or if it has not been pre-shrunk by the manufacturer.

Pin and Cut... Professionally

Select the layout on your Cutting Guide that accords with your pants version, size and fabric width. CIRCLE IT. Then follow the correct procedures as you pin and cut. Listed below are a gathering of professional tips we have assembled especially for you—to guarantee perfect results every time:

- Always fold fabric on straight grain with right sides together.
- Pin fabric every 3" or so along indicated foldline, and all ends and selvages. If necessary, clip selvages every few inches so that fabric lies flat.
- Extend grainline the full length of each pattern piece—and measure to selvage at 6" intervals to check the grain-perfect placement of your pattern.
- Double-check all pattern adjustments: see that seam and cutting lines are re-drawn and all corresponding pieces are altered, including facings.
- Lay out all pattern pieces before you begin cutting.
- Place pattern pieces printed side up unless otherwise indicated by the Cutting Guide. Shaded areas in the layout indicate pieces to be placed printed side down.
- Pin first along lengthwise grainline and center folds of pattern pieces.
- Never let fabric hang over the edge of the cutting surface.
- Place pins perpendicular to and ¼" inside cutting line, and diagonally at pattern corners. Position 3" or 4" apart, or closer for sheer or slippery fabrics.
- When layout shows a pattern piece extending beyond the fabric fold, cut the other pieces first; then unfold the fabric and cut out the remaining pattern piece.
- To avoid fabric distortion, cut "directionally" with the grain.
- NEVER cut out a pattern with pinking shears; limit them to finishing seams during construction. Use long, bent-handled shears, and cut with steady, even slashes.
- Never lift fabric from the table. Keep one hand flat on the pattern piece while cutting.
- Cut notches outward, using the point of your shears; cut groups of notches in continuous blocks for easier matching.
- Use each pattern piece the correct number of times. Pocket, cuff, welt and belt carrier pieces are likely to be repeated.
- Fold the cut pieces softly and lay them on a flat surface.
- Save fabric scraps left from cutting. They are often needed for such things as bound buttonholes, sleeve plackets, and other items not cut from pattern pieces . . . or for testing tension, stitch length and pressing techniques.

Special Fabric Layouts

Mad for plaid pants? Or posh velveteens? Yearning for a jumpsuit of magnificently magnified flowers? Make them yours! But remember, many of these distinctive fabrics require extra attention in laying out pattern pieces. If this is your first experience with the special demands of an unusual fabric, note the following specifics . . . be guided by our suggestions . . . and proceed with a spirit of adventure!

Directional Fabrics

Napped or pile fabrics and one-way prints or weaves have one thing in common: all must be cut according to "With Nap" layouts . . . with the tops of all pattern pieces pointing in the same direction. WHICH direction makes a difference . . . and sometimes the choice is yours, sometimes not. For instance: you can cut with the nap running DOWN for a lighter, shinier look (often preferable for such fabrics as wool broadcloth, velours, etc.). OR, cut with nap running UP for a deeper, richer color (usually most desirable for velvet, velveteen and corduroy).

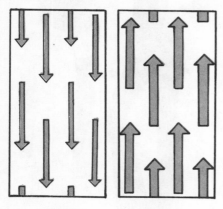

NAP DOWN
LIGHTER

NAP UP
DARKER

Satin and lustrous brocades must also be cut as one-way fabrics, because light reflecting off their surface causes shading effects. And note that on patterns, "nap" applies to any one-way fabric. So when it comes to a one-way-flowering jump, be sure all your posies are poking their heads UP!

Even Plaids and Stripes

The layout techniques for plaids and stripes are basically the same—because a plaid is actually composed of stripes crossing each other at right angles, spaced evenly or unevenly, and repeated in a definite sequence.

Before laying out your pants pattern, note which are the dominant horizontal and vertical stripes of your plaid . . . or the most dominant of your stripes. You will be concerned with the placement of these lines—for figure flattery as well as balance of design. (To discover the most dominant line of your striped fabric, squint at it to see whether the widest stripe, the brightest stripe, or the stripe at the center of the design comes up strongest.)

Fold your fabric along the center of the dominant vertical stripe—or the center of the plaid design. For non-shift accuracy in cutting, pin the fabric layers together along the stripe lines, or along the dominant plaid lines in both directions. When laying out your pattern be sure to:

- Place the predetermined pants hemline along the lower edge of the dominant plaid line or the dominant crosswise stripe.
- Avoid having a heavy dominant horizontal stripe across the fullest part of the hip—or across the waist or bustline of a jumpsuit.
- Position the most dominant vertical stripe down the center front of your trouser leg.

27

Always MATCH SEAMLINES, not the cutting lines. Use notches as "finders" . . . then maneuver pattern so that the symbols along corresponding seamlines of front and back pieces lie on exactly matching points of the fabric motif.

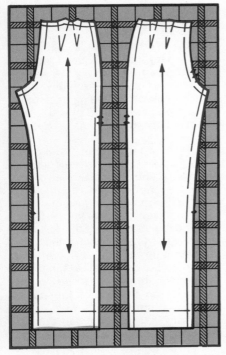

To make matching your plaid just that much easier, draw the plaid on the pattern at matching points.

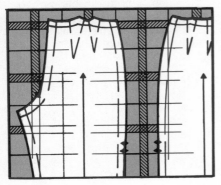

MATCH CENTER SEAMS, both front and back . . . and SIDE SEAMS, whenever possible. Shaped seams should start out in the center of the plaid repeat, or the center of a lengthwise stripe; when seams are joined, the lines will chevron slightly. In flared pants, match OUTSIDE rather than inner leg seamlines.

In laying out a matching top— or a jumpsuit with a waistline seam —be sure to place pattern pieces so that your plaid or stripe design will be continuous and run in the same direction from neck to pants hem.

Once familiar with the principles involved in stripe or plaid layouts, don't be afraid to use these motifs creatively . . . as in a cross or bias cut of pockets, pantleg cuffs or jumpsuit bandings. Or coordinate plaids with checks or stripes—just for the fun of it!

Uneven Plaids and Stripes

These motifs are, truthfully, not for the novice when it comes to making pants. However, in the hands of a skilled, experienced seamstress, they can result in totally great looks! So, IF you are highly capable, plunge into this fashion-sewing adventure . . . and look to the VOGUE SEWING BOOK for detailed guidance in layout and matching.

Choose a pattern with a minimum of seams and construction lines, to reduce the number of matching points. And (just as for even plaids and stripes) determine the dominant lines of the plaid or stripe motif which you will want to emphasize for fashion effect and figure flattery.

In working with uneven vertical stripes, you may create either of two effects: have the stripes move in one direction around the body . . . or have them form a mirror image on both sides of your garment.

Large-Scale and Border Prints

Decide whether your large-scale motif is prominent enough to require matching. And definitely avoid placing large flowers or circles, etc., directly on the bust, tummy or derriere. If your print has a distinct one-way design, use the "With Nap" layout.

Border prints offer opportunities for great creativity...and smashing effects in pant or jumpsuit outfits! If your pattern is not illustrated in a border print, you will have to devise your own layout and buy additional yardage. With lengthwise border prints, fold fabric on the CROSSWISE grain to achieve horizontal bordering on pantlegs, or across the top or bordering the sleeves of a jumpsuit. Place pattern

with pre-determined hemlines along the border—and have all grainline markings along the CROSSWISE grain of the fabric. With experience, you can also work out more complex effects—as, using the border vertically up the sides of the pants.

Underlining

If you are going to underline your pants, cut underlining from the same pattern pieces . . . and transfer all your construction markings onto this underfabric.

Make Your Mark!

If your pants will not be underlined, transfer all pattern markings to the wrong side of your fabric as soon as the garment pieces are cut. Use the marking method most appropriate to your fabric:

1. Tracing Wheel and Dressmaker's Carbon are best for hard-surfaced fabrics. Use a ruler to trace straight lines.

2. Pins and Chalk can be used on soft or hard-surfaced fabrics.

3. Tailor's Tacks are recommended for fabrics which might be marred by other markings . . . and they are a requisite for soft-surfaced fabrics such as velvet, spongy tweeds, wools or blends with napped or nubby faces.

Staystitch all loosely woven or knitted fabrics along curved or bias edges to prevent stretching during construction. Do this as soon as you remove pattern tissues, handling fabric carefully. Use a regulation machine stitch, ½" from raw edges . . . and always staystitch WITH THE GRAIN in the directions shown in diagram and as prescribed for Directional Stitching, page 34. Staystitch pants at waistline, curved sides of hipline, and crotch. Staystitch neckline, shoulders and armholes (if sleeveless) of a jumpsuit.

Thread trace all grainline markings and position lines of High and Full Hip, Knee, etc., to the right side of your fabric. These lines will eliminate guesswork in fittings later; one glance in the mirror, and you'll see just where adjustments or corrections may be needed. If your pants have a center creaseline — thread trace this, too.

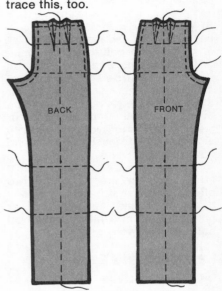

As the front and back pants sections look quite similar, identify both fronts OR both back pieces with small safety pins. (And if you forget which is which, remember: the front is slightly smaller than the back when you line up the inner leg and crotch seams . . . and darts are always shorter in front.)

Underlined Pants

Cut underlining from the same pattern pieces, and transfer all pattern markings to this fabric (instead of your fashion fabric) using a tracing wheel and dressmaker's carbon.

Working on a flat surface, center marked underlining over the wrong side of each fabric section— with grainlines perfectly matched.

Pin fabrics together along grainline markings; smooth outward along lengthwise and crosswise grain and pin together around edges and along center of darts. From here on, treat the two layers of fabric as one.

Staystitch the same as for non-underlined fabric. Thread trace all markings from the underlining side to the right side of your fashion fabric. At seamlines, thread trace next to—not on—the marked lines so the threads will be easy to remove later. (You need not thread trace staystitched seamlines; the staystitching —which will be ⅛" outside seamline markings—will be your guidelines in later construction.)

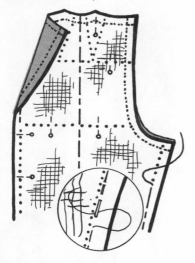

Let's Join Up!

Baste your pants together in preparation for fitting, and as a pre-run of permanent stitching later. Follow the step-by-step continuity on your Sewing Guide. You can baste by hand or machine.

Hand Baste by sewing alongside the seamline in the seam allowance for easy removal of threads later. Use a contrasting color thread and even stitches about ¼" long; begin

and end your basting with backstitches. For particularly firm basting, take a backstitch every few inches . . . and gear length of stitches to the individual fabric and probable strain in try-ons.

Slip Baste for accuracy in matching stripes, plaids, or prints, or for fitting alterations. Crease and turn under the seam allowance of one piece to be joined. With right sides up, lay the folded edge in position over the corresponding piece, matching the fabric design at the seamline; pin. Slip the needle through the upper fold, then through the lower garment section, using ¼" stitches. The result is a plain seam with basting on the wrong side.

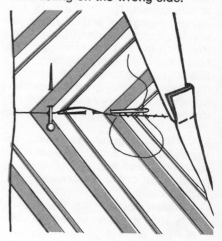

Baste by machine if your fabric is firm, won't slip or show needle marks. Set your machine for the longest stitch and loosen the upper tension slightly so thread is easily removable. To remove, clip the top thread at intervals and pull out the bottom thread. Don't backstitch at seam ends; knot the threads to keep the stitches secure.

Always machine baste pantleg and other seams directionally (see page 34) whenever possible.

The Fitting Things

Your fitting is really a "dress rehearsal" of how your finished pants will look and perform. If you have made all personalized pattern adjustments according to your muslin fitting shell, you will probably find only very minor changes are necessary to perfect and finalize the fit of your pants or jumpsuit now. But it's those little things that count, you know!

Fit To Be Tried

All the major pieces of your garment should be basted together. No need for pant facings, pockets, etc. yet . . . nor for the sleeves or collar of a jumpsuit. But DO baste a temporary grosgrain waistband to the waist seamline of your pants, to properly support them while fitting. Likewise, wear a belt while fitting a belted jumpsuit. Have zipper closing basted under on one side, and marked with colored basting stitches on the other. so you can pin it closed accurately.

Try your garment on with the undergarments and shoes you intend to wear . . . and study yourself before a full-length mirror in a well-lighted room.

Stand naturally. Sit. Bend. Walk. Pants are for action as well as fashion! Can yours high-step it onto a bus or commuter train? Do they take your curves in stride?

Ascertain that your pants provide enough ease and comfort . . . but don't fit so closely that figure flaws become noticeable. Be sure you have adequate length from waist to crotch . . . or from neck to crotch of a jumpsuit. And in the latter, move your arms . . . and note the set of the shoulders. Check the placement of closures and fastenings. Look for any little problems caused by your particular body contours.

The fabric itself often influences the fit of your garment. Wrinkles tattle of grain distortion—or of areas which are too tight or too loose. Learn to understand such wrinklings; smooth them into the correct position to locate their roots...and eliminate them with minor adjustments of a dart or seam.

Seamlines, thread-traced grainlines and position lines are also important fitting guides. Side seams and vertical grainlines should be perpendicular to the floor...horizontal seams and grainlines, parallel to the floor. If any of these are askew, now is the time to bring them into position. To do this, open and repin the seams on your figure. Or—for a faster method—pin or chalk mark new seamlines, and make the changes after removing the garment. (Remember that when you move a seamline, corresponding changes must be made in adjoining section.)

If, at this point there is any excess fullness at the back of your pants...or if you just prefer a tighter fit...note the Back-Fitting Seams technique (page 24). This unique "fashion" alteration could be a successful corrective measure now.

To complete your fitting, baste pants together along corrected seamlines, and try on again before stitching permanently.

Note: The Knit Fit

It is sometimes impossible to know beforehand just how much lengthwise stretch is built into certain knits . . . and more important, just how that stretch will affect the final fit of your pants, particularly in the crotch area. It may be that you will need less body ease, but a little more fabric at the crotch, when your pants are translated into the actual knit fabric. Therefore, FOLLOW THESE SPECIAL STEPS in cutting and fitting your knit pants:

To Cut: Add an extra 2″ or 2½″ to the seam allowance at the lower crotch on both front and back pattern pieces. Taper allowance from the full amount at the point of the crotch to nothing at the notches marking the turn of the curve.

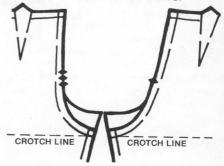

CROTCH LINE   CROTCH LINE

Leave this seam area un-basted until the time of your fitting.

To Fit: Wearing your pants inside out, pin the upper leg seam into correct position, so that it fits smoothly, and pantlegs hang straight and allow ample length while standing and sitting. Mark correct crotch seam with chalk; then remove garment and baste as marked.

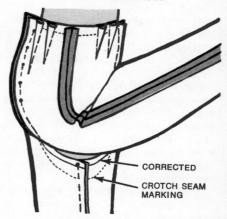

CORRECTED

CROTCH SEAM MARKING

Try on the completely basted pants again for a final fitting check of this seam area before you commence stitching.

Put It All Together

You're ready to sew up some super pants! So right now, get to know the secret of ALL successful fashion sewing. That is: to press as you go . . . as you sew . . . as you complete each stitching step of construction. And this technique is particularly essential to the final professional look of your pants or jumpsuit —where a smooth, sleek effect is especially desired. (So much so, that we'll keep reminding you of this procedure right along with the various steps in completing your pants outfit.)

So—stitch and press . . . stitch and press. Make it a habit! And you'll make the most of all the fine fitting that's gone before—and all the construction steps ahead!

Stitch...Stitch... Stitch!

Before you start, use a scrap of your fabric to test the machine tension and pressure—and determine the correct stitch length.

Most fabrics call for a regular straight machine stitch. However, knits with considerable stretch and recovery are best sewn with a tiny zigzag stitch (if your machine is so geared) to incorporate more stretch in the seams . . . OR use a straight stitch and a 100% polyester or cotton-covered polyester thread which has built-in "give". Both machine pressure and thread tension should be light for knits. And as you stitch, stretch your fabric very slightly on both sides of needle to achieve a smoother seam.

Directional stitching is a technique important to the success of your pants. This means stitching in the direction of the grain (just as in staystitching)—to prevent stretching of the seam areas and ensure smooth joinings. (To determine the direc-

tion of the grain, run your finger along the cut edge of your fabric. The threads with the grain will lie smoothly . . . those against it will come loose and begin to fray.)

WITH THE GRAIN   AGAINST THE GRAIN

In pants or jumpsuits, stitching directionally usually means stitching leg seams from the widest to the narrowest part and bodice seams from neck or underarm to the waistline. Stitch directionally for your zipper installation, too. Basically horizontal seams (as waistline, neckline, collars, etc.) should be stitched directionally from sides to center.

Reinforce the crotch seam curve from notch to notch with a second row of stitching, ¼" from the first, in the seam allowance. Then trim close to this second stitching and overcast both raw edges together by hand. Clip at notches; press seam open above clips. The double-stitched portion of the crotch seam will remain unpressed.

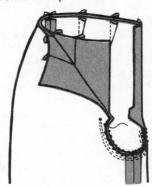

...And Press As You Go!

Along with the all-important procedure of stitch-and-press, observe these general rules for proper pressing:

1. **Test-press** a good-sized scrap of your fabric. See how it reacts to steam, moisture and heat . . . how the pressed portion compares with the unpressed. Gabardines, for instance, can easily develop a shine in pressing.) Velvet, corduroy or deeply ribbed knits will call for a needleboard.

2. **Press with steam.** If you have no steam iron, use a dry iron with a damp press cloth made from several layers of cheesecloth.

3. **Press on the wrong side of your fabric** whenever possible.

With this format established, your path is clear ahead. Begin with the darts. Continue with the major seams, following your pattern's Sewing Guide for the procedure required by your design. And PRESS ALL DARTS AND SEAMS AS YOU GO— so that all intersecting seams will lie smooth and flat.

Darts

Stitch darts from the wide base to nothing at the pointed end—with the last few stitches directly on the fold.

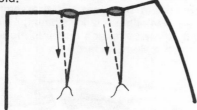

Contour darts (often found in jumpsuits) begin and end with points. Sew the first stitches very slowly to be sure they catch only a few threads of the fabric; clip fold

along curve to release. Secure thread ends at all dart points with a knot rather than backstitching. Tie the knot as shown, working it to the tip of the dart.

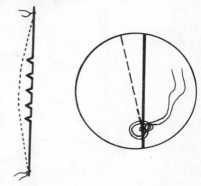

Press darts over the curved surface of a tailor's ham or press mitt to maintain their built-in shaping.

First, press each dart flat, as stitched—but never past the pointed end! Then, on the wrong side of the opened garment, press dart in the proper direction . . . working from the wider end to the point. Press waistline darts toward the center front or back—underarm darts, downward—unless otherwise instructed by your pattern. Slip a strip of brown paper under the dart fold to prevent ridged impressions on the right side of your fabric.

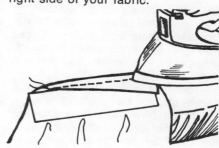

If darts are curved or deep, or if fabric is bulky, slash through center of dart fold to within ½" or 1" of the

35

point—or trim to within ½" of the stitching. Open dart edges with the tip of your iron; then steam press completely open, with the point pressed flat.

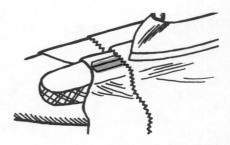

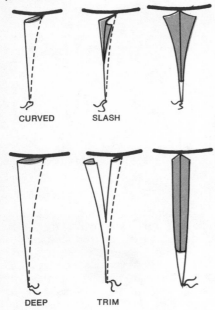

CURVED   SLASH

DEEP   TRIM

Finish by steam pressing the dart and the surrounding garment area to achieve a smoothly contoured effect.

Seams

Basically, all seams are treated alike. First, press along the stitching line to merge stitches with fabric. Open the seam with the tip of your iron . . . then press open. ALWAYS press seams in the direction in which they were stitched.

Straight seams—predominant in pants—should be pressed over a seam roll to avoid ridges showing on the right side . . . OR press them flat on your board, with strips of brown paper slipped under the seam edges. To flatten seams in exceptionally bulky or springy fabric, use a pounding block on the seamline.

Another method of achieving a fine, flattened seamline on especially thick, bulky, or resilient fabrics can be used only on materials which will not be marred by moisture. After opening the seam with the tip of your iron, use a small art brush to "draw" a very fine line of water exactly along the seamline; then press seam open in the usual manner.

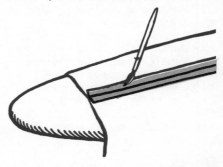

Curved seams should be clipped and pressed flat using the above methods—but they must be done over a curved surface to maintain the built-in roundness of the seam area. Use either a tailor's ham, press mitt or dressmaker's cushion, alone or with a sleeve board.

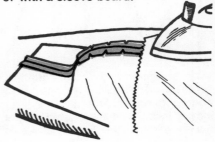

Special Seams

In certain styles—and certain fabrics—it's a fashion plus to let your seams SHOW! Simple techniques and topstitching give these special seams a totally professional look.

Topstitched Seam: Stitch a plain seam; press both seam allowances to one side. Topstitch the desired distance from seam on outside of garment through all thicknesses. For a **Double Topstitched Seam:** Press a plain seam OPEN and topstitch the desired distance from EACH side of seam (not shown).

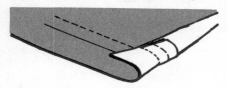

Welt Seam: Stitch a plain seam and press it to one side. Trim the under seam allowance to ¼". Then stitch through only the wider seam allowance and garment, close to—and encasing—the trimmed seam allowance. For a **Double Welt Seam:** Complete a Welt Seam. Then topstitch close to the seam through all thicknesses from the outside of the garment (not shown).

Seam Finishes

The inside story is as important to a great pants look as the outside view. Neatly finished seams will ensure durability, prevent raveling and contribute to the sleekness of silhouette by giving added support to seam allowances.

A variety of seam finishes are suitable to unlined pants. Your choice in this matter should be governed by your fabric—and by the knowledge that pant seam edges are subject to considerable abrasion.

Many knitted, bonded or tightly woven fabrics do not require finishing. Also, if pants are to be fully lined, no finish is necessary unless fabric is exceptionally ravelly. Otherwise, finish seams immediately after pressing.

Machine Zigzag Stitching is the quickest seam finish—and an especially good technique for fabrics that fray easily. If you have a zigzag machine, simply zigzag stitch along each raw edge, using a smaller stitch for lightweight fabrics—a larger one for heavier or bulky types.

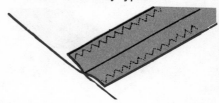

Hand Overcasting is a suitable seam finish for a great majority of fabrics. After seam is pressed open, stitch ¼" from raw edge, then trim to ⅛". Overcast the edge by hand, as shown, using the machine stitching as your guide. (Very firm fabrics can be hand overcast omitting the machine stitching and trimming.)

In some knit fabrics, seams can be finished by just machine stitching ¼" from raw edges, to keep seam allowances from rolling.

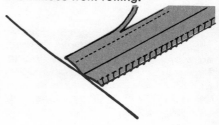

Pinked Seam Edges are a good finish for fabrics which do not ravel. Just trim the raw edges of each seam allowance with pinking shears. For a bit firmer finish, stitch ¼" from each edge before pinking.

The Turned and Stitched seam finish is a good method for lightweight, non-bulky fabrics, including many plain weave synthetics. Turn under the raw edge of seam allowance . . . press if necessary . . . and stitch close to the edge.

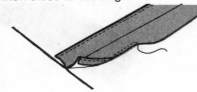

Bound Edges provide a fine, strong finish, especially suitable for heavier fabrics or those that are easily frayed. Use purchased double-fold bias tape to encase each raw edge—placing the slightly narrower fold of the tape on top and edge-stitching through all thicknesses.

This bound edge technique is especially applicable to the crotch area of pants in almost any fabric. The reinforced crotch seam curve will be made doubly durable with this binding rather than overcasting. (See page 34.)

The Close-Ups

With just one possible exception, closure methods used on pants and jumpsuits are not radically different from those used in making other garments. Essentially, you will be dealing with zippers, buttons and buttonholes, and various types of hooks and eyes.

However, there are certain "close-up" considerations that can distinguish your pants project. For example—it's important to choose the closure that will work for you. If you plan to wear a belt or a close-fitting top over your pants, a button closing may get in the way or cause unseemly bumps . . . so you would want to choose a flatter, sleeker waist closure.

Here are some of the ways to make it an open and closed case for pants . . . with great finesse!

Zippers

Zippers call for just a bit of special handling when it comes to pants or jumpsuits. First of all, select a zipper that is compatible with your fabric in weight, suppleness and care requirements. Then determine the best application for your garment, on a basis of eye appeal as well as practicality. Consider your figure, too. Remember, for instance, that center seam closures are preferable to side ones for the lady with curvaceous hips. Follow the application instructions included in your zipper package—and refer to the VOGUE SEWING BOOK for greatly detailed specifics.

Hand Sewn: The custom technique of hand applied zippers is suitable for visible zipper closures that will not receive undue strain—as at the center front of a jumpsuit. To emphasize the positive couture look, try using embroidery floss for your prickstitches, to give them a decorative dimension of their own.

Machine Stitched: No matter how much you may prefer the look of a hand application—machine stitching is a requisite for pant and jumpsuit closures where the zipper will be put under strain.

If you don't appreciate the look of machine stitches, use an invisible zipper with the unique application that makes it just disappear into a seam! And makes for a super-smooth silhouette! Or—especially on jumpsuits—make stitches tell a little fashion story of their own . . . pretty 'em up by sewing them with silk buttonhole twist in your machine, instead of regular thread.

And of course, some jumpsuits —and pants, too—can go all out for the fashion thing when it comes to zippers . . . creatively framed with such goodies as rickrack, soutache, peasant braid—or even jeweled trim!

Fly Front Placket: Remember the closure "exception" mentioned earlier? This is it: the fly placket—a zipper application which you're not apt to encounter too frequently in garments other than pants. And—as closures go—it's perhaps the most distinctive and professional of them all.

We recommend that you use the fly placket only when your pattern is specifically designed for it. Instructions are, of course, given with your pattern—but you may find our detailed guidance helpful if this "close-up" construction is new to you.

Working with a specially designed trouser zipper or a regular zipper, begin by turning in both fly front extensions along the foldlines, and baste close to the folds. Pin or baste the closed zipper under the left front, with the teeth close to the basted edge, and the bottom stop at the bottom of the opening. (Note: the zipper may extend above the opening edges.) Lap the right front extension over the zipper, even with the center

front marking on the left front, and baste it in place.

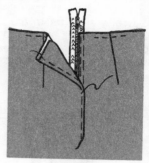

Open out the right front extension and baste the zipper tape to it, being careful not to catch the front of the garment. Stitch the zipper in place close to the teeth, and again ¼" away on the tape.

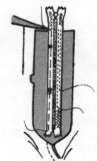

Then turn the extension back and baste it to the garment. On the outside, stitch along the stitching line through all thicknesses.

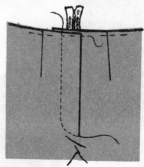

Pull thread to the inside and tie.

Stitch the fly and lining inserts together. Trim, turn and press the seam. Baste the raw edges together. On the wrong side, baste the fly insert to the left front extension over the zipper. Make sure the raw edges are even and the lining faces the inside.

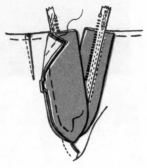

Open the zipper. Keeping the right front free, stitch on the outside through all thicknesses; place your stitches near the zipper teeth and close to the folded edge of the left front. Machine baste along the seamline across zipper tapes so the pull tab will not slide off the end. Trim ends of zipper even with the upper edge if necessary.

Because the base of the opening is subject to strain, secure with a bar tack.

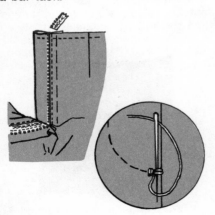

Buttons and Buttonholes

Buttons and buttonholes should be handled with the knowledge that they may be subjected to considerable stress, particularly at the waist. So take steps to reinforce them . . . first of all, from the inside out, with firm interfacing in the closure area.

Sew buttons for strength with buttonhole twist or heavy-duty thread. And always attach with a thread shank—which allows the buttoned fabric to lie smoothly, and avoids pulling. To reinforce buttons on lightly woven or delicate fabrics, place a small folded square of ribbon seam binding directly beneath each one—between facing and garment—and sew through it.

Cording will strengthen buttonholes on heavier fabrics. Machine-worked buttonholes can be reinforced with a second stitching.

Hooks and Eyes

The new latch type hook and eye fastening is perfect for pant waistbands. For a particularly permanent way of attaching these—or regular hooks and eyes—use BUTTONHOLE STITCHES to sew them on, working stitches around the circular holes.

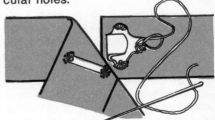

The Inner Beauty

Full linings are more a luxury than a requirement in pants. In most cases, underlinings will provide the necessary stability . . . a smooth underfinish for rough-textured fabrics . . . or the easy "slip" you might want if you are wearing, say, wool shortpants over knit leotards. However, there may be instances when nothing less than the million-dollar feel of a full lining will please you . . . and accomplish all the above, and more! And you'll find that lining pants is a surprisingly easy feat.

Pant Lining

Your lining will be applied when pants have been stitched together, with zipper installed . . . but before the permanent waistband or facing is attached.

Cut lining from the main pieces of your pants pattern. Mark and baste it together, just as you did your pants—making the same, if any, alterations. Leave the appropriate seam open for the zipper.

Then make a fitting check: insert basted lining in pants, wrong sides together; pin together at the waist and along the inner leg seamlines from the outside. Try on pants and lining—checking to see that a smooth fit prevails at waist, hip and crotch, and that pantlegs hang smoothly.

As with all circumferences, the outer layer (pants) should be slightly larger than the inner layer (lining) for both layers to work together compatibly. This fine line of difference can be achieved by minutely decreasing each lining seam. But ON NO ACCOUNT MUST THE LINING BE NOTABLY SMALLER THAN YOUR PANTS; it will distort the fit, be uncomfortable, and cause trouble from beginning to end!

When you are satisfied with the fit, remove lining from pants. Stitch the lining sections together—pressing darts and seams. Then align pants with lining, wrong sides out and together; have closures back to back, and INNER LEG SEAMS MATCHED. Join inner leg seam allowances of pants and lining with long, loose running stitches.

To turn pants and lining right side out, reach through each pant leg, grasp BOTH hemlines, and pull lining through each pant leg to its inside positioning.

Pin pants and lining together at upper edge. Slipstitch lining to the zipper tape—and baste pinned edges of waistline together. Then attach the waistband or waist facing, as instructed by your pattern; this will permanently join lining to pants. Blindstitch facing edges to the lining.

Baste lining to pants along hemline and turn up hem, treating both layers of fabric as one. Sew hem to the lining only. And for a couture touch on your luxuriously lined pants, you may wish to finish your hem with lace seam binding—or use a silky ribbon if yours is a heavier fabric.

Jumpsuit Lining

You may line the lower half of a jumpsuit that has a waistline seam following the same procedure given for pants; the lining would be permanently joined when your lined or unlined bodice is attached to the pants portion.

Or, line the entire jumpsuit—basting lining to neck and armhole edges. Then finish neck and armholes in the usual manner.

Knee Lining

If pants are very slim-fitting . . . or if the nature of your fabric indicates that the knees may stretch out of shape . . . a knee lining is the answer.

Cut two lining sections approximately 10"-12" long and the width of the knee area of your front pants pattern. Finish top and bottom edges by stitching ¼" from the edge and overcasting . . . or by zigzag stitching ¼" from the edge.

For correct placement — try on your pants, inside out, and mark the horizontal center of each knee cap. Center lining sections over markings, and pin in place. Stitch sides of the lining to the front seam allowances, directly next to the seamline. Blindstitch the upper and lower edges to the outer fabric so that your feet won't get caught in the loose edges.

On Top Of It All

The ideal waistband is a combination of perfect fit, good looks and pure comfort. It never stretches out, wrinkles down or folds over. Neither does it put you in a bind . . . nor sink down around your hips. It is sleek, smooth, flat . . . and flattering!

Here are the general rules and regulations — and some "in" techniques—to help you achieve waistband perfection for YOUR pants.

1) Always install your zipper before you apply the waistband, unless otherwise instructed by your pattern. Leave ⅛" plus the seam allowance between the top zipper stop and the raw edge of the waist.

2) Pants are usually eased to the waistband to accommodate the curve of your body directly below the waistband. Therefore, your unfinished garment should measure ½" to 1" more around the waist seamline than the finished waist measurement.

3) Many waistbands require the inner support of interfacing or ribbon seam binding to prevent stretching and maintain their shape. This is particularly true when the fabric is loosely woven . . . or when the waistband is wide or contoured.

4) To eliminate inner bulk, always trim and grade the joining seams, leaving the garment seam allowance widest.

5) Side closings are always on the left. Center back closings are recommended for smooth over-the-hip fit.

6) If waistband is to be overlapped, the top edge overlaps toward the left or the back. The underlap section usually extends at least 1¼".

7) If your pant waistband is fastened with hooks and eyes, place larger hooks at the point of greatest strain.

Straight Waistbands

Straight waistbands are cut on the lengthwise grain for minimum stretch. They can be constructed in many ways, depending upon the type of fabric, your pant style, and the intended wear. Your pattern instructions will most likely cover the traditional method of applying a straight waistband. However, if you are working with a fairly thick or heavy fabric, you may wish to use one of the alternate techniques to reduce bulk.

The Selvage Way: This will reduce the ridge caused by multiple seam allowances at waistline. Simply cut the waistband pattern piece with SEAMLINE of the unnotched edge even with the selvage. The selvage then acts as the finished edge, and is not turned under.

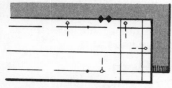

The Ribbon Trick: Achieve a less bulky effect by means of grosgrain ribbon, in the same width as your intended finished waistband. Cut the waistband from your fabric equal to its finished width plus two seam allowances. Lap ribbon over the upper seam allowance on the outside, placing it a scant ⅛″ from seamline, and edgestitch.

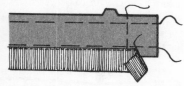

To finish: Both waistbands are finished in the same manner. Fold, right sides together, along foldline or the upper seamline. Stitch across both ends. Trim corners, grade seams, turn and press. Attach to pants, joining notched seams. Slip-stitch selvage or ribbon edge over the seam, continuing across underlap.

Contour Waistbands

To reinforce this shapely banding, interface one of the waistband sections for firmness. Stay the long top and bottom edges of that same section by basting stretched bias tape ⅛″ over seamlines. Join waistband sections; trim and grade seams.

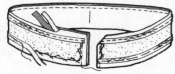

Complete the application of waistband to pants according to your pattern's directions.

Faced Waistlines

This finish—often encountered on low-riding hipsters—is also found on many pants that rise to a normal waistline. It can be a particularly wise choice for the woman whose waist is not as willowy as she might wish—for it eliminates ALL extraneous fabric at the waist.

Cut your facing from lining or lightweight fabric to reduce bulk. Finish lower edge by stitching ¼″ from edge and hand overcasting. Reinforce the facing waist seamline with ribbon seam binding or twill tape, placing one edge ⅛″ over the seamline; baste. Pin facing to pants, easing garment to fit. Stitch, trim, and grade seams. Understitch facing to keep it from rolling to the outside.

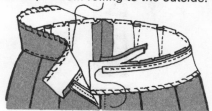

Turn and press. Turn in ends at closure and sew to zipper tape. Tack facing to pant seams and darts. Sew hook and eye at top of closing.

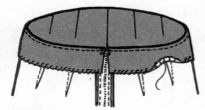

Self Casings

These provide a quick and easy finish at the waistline of simply styled pants where all dart fitting has been eliminated. Especially appropriate for casual, sport, or knitted pants, the casing enables fabric to be snugged into place with elastic—and is particularly comfortable to wear.

A self casing is formed by an extension of the garment that is folded, hem-like, to the inside and edgestitched. To eliminate excess bulk, trim seams which will be inside of casing. Leave casing open at one seam area to insert elastic. Edgestitch along top fold of casing.

The elastic in your casing will ensure regularity of fit — and will move and breathe with you. Make it slightly less than your own waist measurement, plus ½″ for lapping. Pull elastic through casing with a bodkin or a safety pin, being careful not to twist it. Lap the ends ½″ and stitch securely.

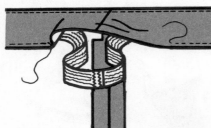

Then close the casing opening, stretching the elastic as you stitch.

Turned-On Hems

A well-made hem is always the least noticeable hem! It should bring your pantlook to a beautiful conclusion with a clean, smooth line. To achieve this ideal, observe these techniques for hem-happy pants:

Take all prescribed steps to eliminate bulk and reduce extra fullness which may exist. Do hand sewing with a light touch, never pulling stitches tightly. And remember that hems are—most importantly—a "pressing matter." So press carefully to prevent ridges and avoid all traces of handling.

Prepare for your hem by checking the final pant length—and pin hem in place wearing the heel height to be worn with the finished pants. Your pant style will dictate where the hem will fall: long, short—or shorter. Note that full length pants should cover the ankle, but never break or bag above shoe tops.

Plain Hem

This is the simplest and most basic of hems. It has little or no fullness—and is apt to be the most generally used hem for pants. The steps taken to complete it are also the preliminary steps to most hems.

After marking your hemline, trim any seam allowances below it to ¼″ —eliminating bulk that could show up when hem is pressed. Then turn hem up and baste close to fold; measure hem depth, and trim evenly.

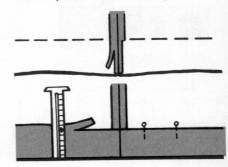

Press the hem with brown paper between hem and pantleg, steaming out any fullness. Avoid pressing over basting threads. Finish raw edge in the way best suited to your pants style and fabric (see Hem Finishes, page 46). Sew hem in place. Then remove basting, and steam press again. Use a pounding block if a crisp hem edge is desired.

Eased Hem

This type hem—found on flared pantlegs—involves excess fullness that must be adjusted. To accomplish this, make the hem about 1"-2" deep, then easestitch ¼" from raw edge, using long machine stitches. Pull up the ease thread every few inches. Then place brown paper between fabric layers, and shrink out hem fullness with a steam iron. To do this, hold iron ABOVE hem and allow steam to do its work in reducing the excess fabric.

Finish the raw edge and sew as suggested for the Plain Hem.

In the case of wide, circular-flared pantlegs, allow pants or jumpsuit to hang for 24 hours before the final hem marking. Then complete, following the above Eased Hem steps.

Double-Stitched Hem

This hem is ideal for knits and heavyweight fabrics. Turn hem up as usual, shrink and adjust any ease. Stitch and overcast the raw edge. Next, baste along the center of the hem. Fold hem back along the basting and catchstitch to pantleg. (This line of stitching is for support only; do not pull the stitches too tightly.) Turn up the top edge of the hem and sew it with a second line of loose catchstitching. Remove bastings and steam press.

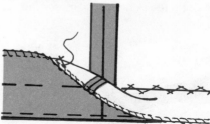

Interfaced Hem

A soft pants or jumpsuit style— or the soft material from which it's made—could require the control of this special type hem to achieve a smooth, unbroken line. To make this, begin by thread tracing the determined hemline. Then, using regular interfacing fabric for body—or lamb's wool for a softer effect—cut 2 bias strips, each the width of one pantleg hem and long enough to lap ½" at ends. Piece if necessary, and pre-shape the interfacing to correspond with the curve of your hem. Place strip over hemline with one edge extending ⅝" below the thread tracing. Sew to garment with long running stitches along the hemline and long catchstitches along the upper edge. Then turn hem up and baste close to the fold. Finish raw edge as desired. Blindstitch hem to pantleg, easing fullness if necessary.

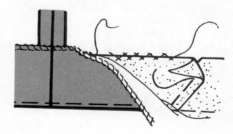

Soft Hem

When it comes to pressing, a gently rolled hem edge may be preferred. To achieve this, simply hold the iron 2"-3" from the hem, steaming the fabric thoroughly—but never resting the iron directly on the fabric.

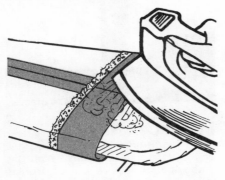

Pat LIGHTLY with a pounding block or ruler to mold hem. Let garment dry thoroughly before wearing.

Hem Finishes

Your choice of hem finish should depend upon the fabric as well as the style, purpose and care requirements of your pants or jumpsuit.

Seam Binding is best for fabrics which tend to ravel—and for machine washable garments. Use ribbon seam binding for straight hems (or add the couture touch of ribbon, lace or braid). Use bias seam binding or stretch lace for eased and circular hems.

Turned-and-Stitched finishes are suitable for straight hems on casual cottons or light and medium weight washable fabrics.

Stitched and Overcast or **Stitched and Pinked** finishes—both, flat and bulkless—are good finishes for fully lined pants and jumpsuits.

To Sew, use a slipstitch or hemming stitch for turned-and-stitched or seam binding finish . . . a blindstitch for pinked or overcast finishes.

Cuffs

Cuffs may turn up on any of many pant styles—providing a fashion flip all their own. And—with a bit of ingenuity—you can ADD them to a cuffless design! But you'll have to start the transformation back at the pattern-adjustment and cutting-out stage. At that time, remember to LENGTHEN the pattern leg BY TWICE THE DESIRED CUFF DEPTH. Then, when you reach this final stage, complete hems as usual—and turn them up, as cuffs, along the hemline markings. Press to a crisp finish, using a pounding block. Catch cuff to pantleg at side seams with a French Tack.

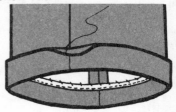

The Final Touches

Time for the final pressing! And if you've followed the "press-as-you-go" principles of construction, this step—with but one exception—should be merely a touch-up job at this point.

The exception occurs if your pants are to be trouser-creased. If so, you'll want these lines to be arrow-straight, crisp and clean. To properly place creases, fold each pantleg so that the side seam and inner leg seam are perfectly aligned. The fold lines thus formed will be your trouser creaselines: from hip to hem at front . . . from crotch level to hem at back. (And make sure that these lines follow the grain of your fabric.) Press with steam AND a damp presscloth, to avoid the risk of shine—and use a pounding block to achieve knife-sharp creases.

Lay pants on a flat surface until they are thoroughly dry.

To ensure the most ENDURING creases—and add a fashion note, in the bargain—you may wish to edge-stitch along the front creaselines.

As for the final touch-up pressing: soft waistline pleats, jumpsuit collars or other areas that need "setting" should be pressed with the garment on a hanger. (Clip pants to hanger by waistband for this step.) Then simply steam and pat these areas into position without touching iron to fabric.

Show You Care!

The care you give your pants between wearings will be reflected in their great good looks when they're out on view, on You!

Give them the right hang-ups! The weight of your fabric, as well as your pant or jumpsuit style are the factors to consider when deciding how to hang them. The idea is to keep the garment in shape and avoid undue strain while it is "off duty."

Most straight-leg pants should be hung by their hemlines, clipped to a special pants hanger—with the pantlegs folded so that side seams and inner leg seams are aligned. In the case of very bulky fabrics, many

knits or sheer fabrics—align pantlegs and then fold pants over the crossbar of a padded hanger.

Jumpsuits can be hung on regular dress hangers—or folded, with pantlegs aligned, over a padded hanger.

In the case of particularly stretchy knits, slinky tricot jumpsuits, and such—disregard hangers entirely. Just fold them carefully with pantlegs evened as usual—and keep them in a dresser drawer or a closet shelf.

In laundering or dry cleaning, follow any hangtag instructions which may have been provided with your fabric. Or be guided by the excellent "Fiber and Fabric Facts" chart in the VOGUE SEWING BOOK —as well as the detailed "Spot Removal" chart in that same book.

Your pants have been lavished with the best of everything! In the planning ... the fitting ... the making ... the final care. And they show it! Wear them proudly ... and ENJOY!

Index